JUMP FOR JOY

MORE RAPS & RHYMES

SUSAN HILL

ELEANOR CURTAIN
PUBLISHING

First published in Australia 1993

ELEANOR CURTAIN PUBLISHING
906 Malvern Road
Armadale 3143

The National Library of Australia
Cataloguing in Publication Data

Hill, Susan (Susan Elizabeth).
Jump for joy: more raps and rhymes.

ISBN 1 875327 17 7

1. Nursery rhymes, English — Study and teaching
(Primary). I. Title.

372.64044

Produced by Sylvana Scannapiego, Island Graphics
Designed by Antoinette Monteleone-Gustini — Optima Design
Illustrated by Mitch Vane
Edited by Sara Curtain
Graphic Services by Optima Typesetting & Graphic Design
Printed by Impact Printing (VIC) Pty Ltd

Leisure & Community Services

Please return this item by the last date stamped below, to the library from which it was borrowed.

Renewals
You may renew any item twice (for 3 weeks) by telephone or post, providing it is not required by another reader. *Please quote the number stated below.*

Overdue charges
Please see library notices for the current rate of charges for overdue items. Overdue charges are not made on junior books unless borrowed on adult tickets.

Postage
Both adult and junior borrowers must pay any postage on overdue notices.

	CJR STAFF COPY		
	NOT FOR LOAN		

739.96

THE LONDON BOROUGH

Contents

Chants with Two Parts

Chants for More Voices

Absolute Nonsense

Introduction

These chants or poems for reading aloud were selected because they make us smile. Sometimes we smile because of the humour, the twists or word play. Sometimes it's the rhythm or rhyme that amazes us. School will always be a serious place of learning but these chants can serve two purposes — both learning and fun.

The educational purposes of raps, chants and rhymes:
Many of these chants began as popular street rhymes and bring the fun of children's clapping games into the classroom. Children will recognise parts of these chants in popular songs, and remember some of the rhymes from the very early years. Using raps, chants and rhymes helps bring together the outside play culture and the school culture. I can't separate the 'fun' purposes from the 'learning' purposes for using raps, chants and rhymes. When groups of students read, clap and chant together a group magic occurs.

A spirit of group cohesion:
The group becomes united, a spirit of cohesion, or co-operation is created. People help each other read and join in. Children are prompted to read. If participants clap, bang percussion instruments, click fingers or make weird sound effects the magic works better.

Voices can be used to create music or dramatic effect.

Inventing an echo like 'This train don't carry no stealers, **(this train)**' encourages students to use polyphony or group harmonising of voices. We don't always want to be predictable in our harmonising and so adding a new sound effect or creating a new rhythm or new words enables these chants to continue to grow and change.

Group chants for reading practice:
These chants are easy to read and can be reread many times. Groups read and reread as they work out ways to read the chant for themselves, to perform for other groups or to perform for other classrooms. Readers who require frequent repetitions when reading a text receive this practice. The group usually reads together so less proficient readers receive the support of their peers.

More proficient readers may explore the way the rhythm and rhyme encourage us to predict and read on. Different ways of performing and changing the text can be explored. All readers like to innovate and add their suggestions for ways to improve the text or make suggestions about the way the group is reading.

Where to find chants:
To find the chants I went to collections of folk tales, folk songs, street games and chants from many cultures and languages. I sifted through recent anthologies of poems and chants. I searched through collections of spirituals and collections of the blues. I searched for over two years. Usually whenever work became too serious I would set time aside to read old chants and rhymes.

I found rhythms and rhymes I had heard before in the jazz and rock music of the sixties and seventies. I found rhythms and rhymes like —

'Baby please don't go,
Baby please don't go
Baby please don't go
Down to New Orleans . . .'

and

'See, see rider
Come and see what you have done.'

These old blues chants often had an adult unrequited love theme and were not included. Decisions were made not to include chants that were derogatory of gender and race, I think that there are enough of these in playgrounds without adding to them. Any that had a taunting, competitive theme were left out. It was difficult to find chants, other than those in English, that could be adapted for classroom use. I am still searching.

Many of the chants, rhymes and rhythms are old. The words have been around for decades. Some very old chants like 'Chicken in the Bread Tray' and 'Zing, Zing, Zing' were included because they have been recreated in several new versions. Children may compare the different versions.

Other chants were found in collections of children's street games and chants like Apples on a Stick from black American children. The folklore collected by the Opies was also used to gather chants from the United Kingdom. Variations of chants from England and Australia were found in song books and collections of poetry.

Many popular poems have the same elements as the old chants and folk lore — rhythm, rhyme and humour which is often nonsense, at times the humour is a little tragic and at times revolting. Children and many of us as adults like language that reminds us not to take ourselves too seriously.

Using the chants:
The chants can be rewritten on large cardboard or paper charts. Different coloured pens show readers where to join in. Most of the chants have suggestions for how to perform the chants. The following techniques would work with any of the chants —

- clap or click to the beat
- use hand clapping combinations like:

○ = clap partner's hands together
● = clap own hands together
L = clap partner's left hand with your left hand
R = clap partner's right hand with your right hand.

The children have more complicated versions of these clapping games so they will make suggestions.

- use a lead voice and a group voice to follow
- divide the class into sections group A, group B, group C and so on.
- assign readers like reader 1, reader 2, reader 3, reader 4 for each character or line of a chant.

The chants are for children and teachers to change, extend and to innovate and create new verses.

They have the best features of chants that have developed from time tested oral chants and stories. They have rhyme, rhythm and a way to connect and bring a group together through humour, hope and a message that whatever life may bring us, the human spirit will play, clap and triumph!

Storytelling Rap

This rap has a caller who asks a question and a response for a group to shout. Most of the rap is read or spoken by one rapper. You could arrange the rap so that several readers take different parts.

CALLER   Have you heard?
RESPONSE   SPREAD THE WORD!
CALLER   Have you heard?
RESPONSE   SPREAD THE WORD!

Yeah, storytelling is the thing to do
It's an ancient art
It's also brand new.
Medicine for the spirit
Healing for the soul
It's for the young
And it's for the old.
It's for the rich
And it's for the poor
For the sick at heart
And what's more
It's for Black people
White people, Brown people too
Red, Yellow, Orange
Green, Purple and Blue.
From the break of day
Till the cool midnight
I can weave a tale
That's outta sight.
Yeah, storytelling is what I'm about
I can run my mouth
Till my eyes pop out.

CALLER   *Have you heard?*
RESPONSE   *Have you heard?*
CALLER   *SPREAD THE WORD!*
RESPONSE   *SPREAD THE WORD!*

Listen good people
All over the world
Start telling stories

Start spreading the word.
In the tradition
Is a natural condition
You just pass it down
Hand it around.
It's mythical, it's history
It's magical, it's mystery.
Use your imagination
Talk about your dreams
Talk about your heroes
Plans and schemes.
Talk about your family
Life or love
Talk about the spirit
up above.
Talk about the birds
Talk about the bees
Talk about the zebras
Talk about the trees.
A little common sense
A little sense of humour
Let it all hang out
But don't drop your bloomers.

CALLER   *Have you heard?*
RESPONSE *Have you heard?*
CALLER   *SPREAD THE WORD!*
RESPONSE *SPREAD THE WORD!*

Tell the truth, snaggle tooth
What's your story, morning glory?
You don't miss your water
Till your well runs dry.
Anansi is a trickster
Brother Rabbit is sly.
Bocka booka bocka booka bocka bam bam bam.

Bocka booka bocka booka bocka bam bam bam.
Bocka booka bocka booka bocka bam bam bam.
Bocka booka bocka booka bocka bam bam bam.

Claps and Clicks

These chants have a simple 4/4 beat. Participants may clap or click on the beat.

There is a School

This is a clapping and clicking chant. Click first then clap on the beat. Add the name of your school on the first line and discuss where the claps and clicks should go.

In .... , *(your school name)*

There is a school,

And in that school,

There is a class,

And in that class,
There is a desk,
And in that desk
There is a book,
And on that book,

There is a cover
And on that cover
There is a name,
And that name is
....

(Call out your name. Everyone will call a different name making a huge noise. Alternatively choose to call out a person nominated by the group.)

When I was Young

This is a clapping or clicking chant. When chanting the last verse chant very loud on the words in bold type.

●   ●
When I was young
  ●   ●
I had no sense.
   ●   ●
I bought a fiddle
   ●   ●
For 50 cents.
The only tune
That I could play
Was over the hills
And far away.

So **early** in the **morning**
So **early** in the **morning**
So **early** in the **morning**
Before the **break** of **day**.

Food

Tony Bradman

All chant the chorus which is written in bold type. Claps can accompany the chant. ● = clap. Add claps throughout the chant when the beat becomes obvious.

●   ●
I like breakfast
●   ●
I like tea
●   ●
I like putting
  ●   ●
Food in me

I like cornflakes
I like toast
But I like my eggs
The most.

Slice the top off
Poke about
Pull the dripping
Yolk right out.

I like breakfast
I like tea
I like putting
Food in me.

There Was an Old Woman

This is a chant for partner or group clapping games.
☆ *= click* ● *= clap. Add claps and clicks to all verses.*

      ☆   ☆
There was an old woman
      ☆   ☆
Lived under the stairs.
☆   ☆   ☆   ☆
Hee-haw, hee-haw.
☆   ☆
She sold apples,
    ☆   ☆
And she sold pears.
☆ ☆ ●
Hee-haw-hum.
All her bright money
She laid on the shelf.
Hee-haw, hee-haw.
If you want any more
You can sing it yourself.
☆ ☆ ●
Hee-haw-hum.

Old Joe Clarke

● = *hand clap* ○ = *clap partner's hand.*

   ●   ○   ●   ○
Old Joe Clarke, he had a house,
 ●   ○   ●   ○
Was fifteen stories high,
   ●   ○   ●   ○
And every darn room in that house
 ● ○   ●   ○
Was full of chicken pie.

I went down to Old Joe Clarke's
And found him eating supper,
I stubbed my toe on the table leg
And stuck my nose in the butter.

I went down to Old Joe Clarke's
But Old Joe Clarke wasn't in,
I sat right down on the red-hot stove
And got right up again.

Old Joe Clarke had a candy box
To keep his sweetheart in,
He'd take her out and kiss her twice
And put her back again.

Miss Polly

This clapping chant has a clap or click on each beat. When the words are in bold type clap loudly on each word.
☆ = *click* ● = *clap.*

     ☆   ☆
Miss Polly had a dolly

●   ●   ●
Who was **sick, sick, sick,**
   ☆   ☆
So she called for the doctor
    ●   ●   ●
To come **quick, quick, quick.**

The doctor came
With his **bag and his hat,**
and he knocked on the door
With a **rat-tat-tat!**

He looked at the dolly
And he **shook his head,**
He said, 'Miss Polly,
Put her **straight to bed.'**

He wrote on a paper
For a **pill, pill, pill.**
'I'll be back in the morning
With my **bill, bill, bill.**

My Mother Said

This is a clapping chant ●   ○   ●   ○.
● = *clap own hands,* ○ = *clap partner's hands.*

  ● ○ ●   ○
My mother said,
●○ ●   ○
I never should,
  ●   ○ ●   ○
Play with the gypsies
● ○ ●○
In the wood;
If I did she would say,

'Naughty girl to disobey.
Your hair won't curl,
And your eyes won't shine,
You gypsy girl,
You shan't be mine!'
And my father said
That if I did
He'd rap my head
With a teapot lid.
The wood was dark,
The grass was green,
In came Sally
With a tambourine.
I went to sea —
No ship to get across;
I paid ten shillings
For a blind white horse;
I sat on his back
And was off in a crack,
Sally, tell my mother
I shall never come back!

The Farmer

To begin this chant, clap a rhythm 'bum-pe-ty, bum-pe-ty, bump! bum-pe-ty, bum-pe-ty, bump!' or 1,2,3 — 1,2,3 — 1 — 1,2,3 — 1,2,3 — 1. Once you have the rhythm then divide the group in two. Half can chant the words and the other half the Bumpety and Lumpety lines. Both groups can continue clapping the rhythm 1,2,3 — 1, 1,2,3 — 1 on the Bumpety and Lumpety lines.

●　　　●

A farmer went a-trotting
●　　　●
Upon his grey mare,
Bumpety, bumpety, bump!

●   ●

With his daughter behind him
  ●   ●

So rosy and fair
Lumpety, lumpety, lump!

A magpie called 'Caw'
And they all tumbled down.
Bumpety, bumpety, bump!
The mare broke her knees
And the farmer his crown,
Lumpety, lumpety, lump!

The mischievous magpie
Flew laughing away,
Bumpety, bumpety, bump!
And vowed he would serve them
The same the next day,
Lumpety, lumpety, lump!

Beeswax

*This is a clapping game with partners. They clap both hands
together on ● then clap both partner's hands on ○. Chant
loudly on the words in bold type.*

● ○   ●   ○

Beeswax and turpentine
●   ○   ● ○

Make the best of plaster,
  ●   ○   ●   ○

The more you try to pull it off,
  ●   ○   ● ○

It's sure to stick the faster.
I'll buy a horse and hire a gig,

15

And all the world shall have a jig:
And you and I'll do all we can

To **push** the business on,
To **push** the business on;
And we'll do all that ever we can
To **push** the business on.

Engine, Engine, Number Nine

*This could be chanted as a clapping chant or pairs of
children can clap hands together. The hand clapping
pattern may be ● ○ ● ○ ● ○ ● ○ or the pattern may be
● L ● R, ● L ● R, ● L ● R and on the very last line
● L ● R ○.*

○ = partners together,
● = own hands together,
L = left hands together,
R = right hands together.

Engine, engine number nine,
Running on the Chicago line.
When she's polished, she will shine.
Engine, engine, number nine.

Engine, engine number nine,
Running on the Chicago line.
If the train should jump the track,
Do you want your money back?

Engine, engine number nine,
Running on the Chicago line.
See it sparkle, see it shine,
Engine, engine, number nine.

If the train should jump the track,
Will I get my money back?
Yes, no,
Maybe so.

I Went to the River

This is a clapping game with partners. Try to invent clapping patterns where the last three repeated words have partner's hands clapping both together. ● = clap own hands, ○ = clap both partner's hands. The pattern is

● ○ ● ○ ○ ○

● ○ ● ○ ○ ○
I went to the river, river, river,
● ○ ● ○ ○ ○
And I couldn't get across, 'cross, 'cross,
● ○ ● ○ ○ ○
And I paid five dollars, dollars, dollars,
● ○ ● ○ ○ ○
For the old grey horse, horse, horse.

And the horse wouldn't pull, pull, pull,
I swapped him for a bull, bull, bull,
And the bull wouldn't holler, holler, holler,
I swapped for a dollar, dollar, dollar.

And the dollar wouldn't spend, spend, spend,
I put it in the grass, grass, grass
And the grass wouldn't grow, grow, grow,
I got my hoe, hoe, hoe.

And the hoe wouldn't chop, chop, chop,
I took it to the shop, shop, shop,
And the shop made money, money, money,
Like the bees made honey, honey, honey.

See that yonder, yonder, yonder,
In the jay-bird town, town, town,
Where all the women got to work, work, work,
Till the sun goes down, down, down.

Well I eat my meat, meat, meat,
And I gnaw my bone, bone, bone,
Well goodbye honey, honey, honey,
I'm going on home.

Games and Actions

These chants have actions to accompany them. Some actions are suggested but participants may invent their own.

Teddy Bear

This is a traditional skipping game that involves a group chant and actions. The whole group can do the actions.

ALL   Teddy Bear, Teddy bear
Touch the ground   (Action)
Teddy Bear, Teddy Bear
Turn around
Teddy Bear, Teddy Bear
Shine your shoes
Teddy Bear, Teddy Bear
That will do
Teddy Bear, Teddy Bear
Go upstairs
Teddy Bear, Teddy Bear
Say your prayers
Teddy Bear, Teddy Bear
Turn off the light
Teddy Bear, Teddy Bear
Say good night.

Zing, Zing, Zing

This is a circle game. Each player is given a number and sits or stands in a circle. The group claps a 4/4 beat. When his or her number is called by the leader the person calls out without missing a beat. If the person loses the beat or makes a mistake their number cannot be called for three turns. Change leaders after five turns. Players use stylised inflection to accompany the rhythmic clapping.

ALL TOGETHER	One, two, three and a zing, zing, zing.
LEADER	Number one
NUMBER ONE	Who, me?
LEADER	Yes, you.
NUMBER ONE	Couldn't be.
LEADER	Then who?
NUMBER ONE	Number five.
NUMBER FIVE	Who, me?
LEADER	Yes, you
NUMBER FIVE	Couldn't be.
LEADER	Then, who?
NUMBER FIVE	Number nine.
NUMBER NINE	Who, me?
LEADER	Yes, you.
NUMBER NINE	Couldn't be.
LEADER	Then who?
NUMBER NINE	Number two.
NUMBER TWO	Who, me?
LEADER	Yes, you.
NUMBER TWO	Couldn't be.
LEADER	Then, who?
NUMBER TWO	Number four
NUMBER FOUR	Who, me?
LEADER	Yes, you.

and so on . . .

Tennessee Wig Walk

This chant is a skipping game that can be chanted and acted out as an action rhyme. Participants place elbows out to make duck wings and place hands on the ribcage. Flap wings on the beat.

I'm a bow legged chicken,

I'm a knock-kneed sparrow:

I've been that way

Since I don't know when.

You walk with a wiggle
And a squiggle and a squark.
Doing the Tennessee wig-walk.

(do the actions)
Put you toes together
And your knees apart;
Bend your back
And get ready to start.

You flap your elbows
Just for luck,
And you wiggle
And you squaggle
Like a baby duck.

Nabisco

☆ click fingers   ● clap hands   stamp feet
head from side to side   hips from side to side

☆   ☆
I have a boyfriend
☆ ☆
Nabisco
☆   ☆
He's so sweet
☆ ☆
Nabisco
Like a cherry tree
Nabisco
Ache ache and a boom do boom
I need some money
And I need it soon
So let's get the rhythm of the hands
●   ●
Clap clap
Now we've got the rhythm of the hands
Clap clap
Now let's get the rhythm of the feet
Stomp stomp
Now we've got the rhythm of the feet
Stomp stomp
Now let's get the rhythm of the head
Ding dong
Now we've got the rhythm of the head
Ding dong
Now let's get the rhythm of the hips
Hot dog
Now we've got the rhythm of the hips
Hot dog
Now let's get the rhythm of Nabisco
Clap clap
Stomp stomp

Ding dong
Now we've got the rhythm of Nabisco
Hot dog!

This the Way You Will a Be

This chant has two groups of readers. The group can stand in two long lines facing each other but still able to glance at the chant written on a chart if they forget the words. The group steps out the song by stepping backwards but not really moving. The action looks like a moonwalk as the body appears to move back but the feet slide forward so the two lines remain quite close to each other. Step back on the beat.

      ●   ●
GROUP A This the way you will a be
      ● ●
GROUP B Will a be will a be
      ●   ●
GROUP A This the way you will a be
      ● ●
GROUP B All night long

      Oh step back Sally
      Sally Sally
      Oh step back Sally
      All night long

Oh walking through the alley
Alley alley
Walking through the alley
All night long.

Oh here come another one
Just like the other one
Here comes another one
All night long.

This the way you will a be
Will a be will a be
This the way you will a be
All night long.

A Sailor Went to Sea, Sea, Sea

This action chant is loved by children because of the rhythm and the word play. Chant as a whole group and invent actions for each word repeated.

Oh, a sailor went to sea, sea, sea   *(shield eyes with hand)*
To see what he could see, see, see
But all that he could see, see, see
Was the bottom of the deep blue sea, sea, sea.

Oh, a sailor went to chop, chop, chop   *(make an action as if you*
To see what he could chop, chop, chop *are chopping wood)*
But all that he could chop, chop, chop
Was the bottom of the big blue chop, chop, chop.

Oh, a sailor went to ooh washy wash   *(washing the*
To see what he could ooh washy wash   *clothes action)*
But all that he could ooh washy wash
Was the bottom of the big blue ooh washy wash.

Oh, a sailor went to Timbuctoo *(make a wiggling hip action)*
To see what he could Timbuctoo
But all that he could Timbuctoo
Was the bottom of the big blue Timbuctoo.

Oh, a sailor went to sea, sea, sea   *(Speed up the chant and*
Chop chop chop   *use actions for each word)*
Ooh washy wash
Timbuctoo.

To see what he could see, see, see
Chop chop chop
Ooh washy wash
Timbuctoo.

But all that he could see, see, see
Chop chop chop
Ooh washy wash
Timbuctoo.

Was the bottom of the big blue sea, sea, sea
Chop chop chop
Ooh washy wash
Timbuctoo.

Chants With Two Parts

These chants have two parts. The chants may be read by a lead voice and a group voice. Alternatively two groups in the classroom can read.

Chocolate Goo

1	One two
2	Chocolate goo
1	Three, four
2	Want some more
1	Five, six
2	Pudding mix
1	Seven, eight
2	Bring your plate
1	Nine, ten
ALL	Hungry again

Five Little Sausages

*This chant can be read in two parts with one group reading one line and another group the next line. A student can jump up and say **pop** and four jump up on **bang**.*

Five little sausages,
Frying in a pan,
One went **pop**,
And the others went **bang!**

Eachy Peachy Pearly Plum

Divide into two groups and read a line each. On the last line clap the letters out loud.

GROUP A   Eachy peachy pearly plum
GROUP B   I spy Tom Thumb —
                Tom Thumb in the wood
                I spy Robin Hood —
                Robin Hood in the cellar
                I spy Cinderella —
                Cinderella at the ball
                I spy Henry Hall —
                Henry Hall in the house
                I spy Mickey Mouse —
                Mickey Mouse on the stairs
                I spy the three bears —
                Three bears up a tree
                I spy Humpty Dumpty —
                Humpty sits on and on
                I spy Michael Jackson
                Michael Jackson is a
                S * T * A * R

Spell and clap STAR

This chant is made up of rhyming couplets. Children could create their own version of this chant. When they run out of rhyming words finish with the line . . . is a s-t-a-r.

Feeding The Family

Brian Patten

Read this chant in two groups and all join in on the chorus.

GROUP A   Frog-spawn pie! Frog-spawn pie!
GROUP B   When I feed it to my sister
ALL   **It makes her cry.**

Custard and fish! Custard and fish!
When I feed it to my brother
He's sick in his dish.

Slug-and-worm jam! Slug-and-worm jam!
When I feed it to the baby
It jumps out of the pram.

Garlic jelly! Garlic jelly!
When I feed it to my father
His breath goes smelly.

Rice and rat! Rice and rat!
When I feed it to my mother
She's sick on the cat.

I want to be an astronaut!
I want to write a book!
I don't want to be a ballerina,
Or a cook!

My Little Sister

Tony Bradman

This chant is spoken by a lead voice or small group of readers. A large group joins in on the words written in capital letters.

LEAD   My little sister's got the loudest
         scream in our school. She loves
ALL   SCREAMING

when she falls over in the playground
and hurts herself you can hear her
SCREAMING

five whole streets away. No one
except me can get her to stop
SCREAMING

once she's started. My dad says it
sounds like a riot. So while she's
SCREAMING

a teacher comes to fetch me
and I have to try and stop her
SCREAMING.

I love my little sister but
I just wish sometimes she was more
QUIET.

28

Pizza, Pizza, Daddy-o!

This two part chant was created by children from a school in Philadelphia, U.S.A.

CALLER:	(Jimmy) is having a birthday party.
RESPONSE:	Pizza, pizza, daddy-o!
CALLER:	How do you know?
RESPONSE:	Pizza, pizza, daddy-o!
CALLER:	Cause I saw it!
RESPONSE:	Pizza, pizza, daddy-o!
CALLER:	Let's jump it!
RESPONSE:	Jump it, jump it, daddy-o!
CALLER:	Let's shake it
RESPONSE:	Shake it, shake it, daddy-o!
CALLER:	Let's hop it!
RESPONSE:	Hop it, hop it, daddy-o!
CALLER:	Let's twist it!
RESPONSE:	Twist it, twist it, daddy-o!
CALLER:	Let's monkey it!
RESPONSE:	Monkey it, monkey it, daddy-o!
CALLER:	Let's boogie it!
RESPONSE:	Boogie it, boogie it, daddy-o!

Repeat the whole chant using a different child's name.
Apparently 'monkey' refers to a rhythm and blues dance.
Ask the class to find out how to 'monkey'.

This Train

Tim Hood

This chant has two parts. One half of the group chants the plain text and one half chants the bold text. All clap or click to keep the beat at a constant rhythm.

This train don't carry no stealers, **this train,**
This train don't carry no stealers, **this train,**
This train don't carry no stealers,
Of pencils, rubbers or two wheelers,
This train don't carry no stealers, **this train.**

This train has all you need now, **this train,**
This train has all you need now, **this train,**
This train has all you need now,
Love and sharing, there's no greed,
This train has all you need now, **this train.**

This train don't carry no fears, **this train,**
This train don't carry no fears, **this train,**
This train don't carry no fears,
No fights, no wars, not even tears,
This train don't carry no fears, **this train.**

This train don't carry no cheaters, **this train,**
This train don't carry no cheaters, **this train,**
This train don't carry no cheaters,
Liars, whingers, nasty creatures,
This train don't carry no cheaters, **this train.**

This train has all you need now, **this train,**
This train has all you need now, **this train,**
This train has all you need now,
Love and sharing, there's no greed now,
This train has all you need now, **this train.**

Them Bones Gonna Rise Again

This chant works well with a lead voice reading the text and the rest of the group joining in on the chorus. The group reading the chorus stands up each time they chant and raise and shake their hands over their heads.

LEAD VOICE   In come the animals two by two:
                       Hippopotamus and a kangaroo;
GROUP VOICE **Them bones gonna rise again!**

                       In come the animals three by three:
Two big cats and a bumble bee;
Them bones gonna rise again!

In come the animals four by four:
Two through the window, and two through the door;
Them bones gonna rise again!

In come the animals five by five:
Almost dead and hardly alive;
Them bones gonna rise again!

In come the animals six by six:
Three with clubs and three with sticks;
Them bones gonna rise again!

In come the animals seven by seven:
Four from hell and the others from heaven;
Them bones gonna rise again!

In come the animals eight by eight;
Four on time, and the others late;
Them bones gonna rise again!

In come the animals nine by nine:
Four in front and five behind;
Them bones gonna rise again!

In come the animals ten by ten:
Five big roosters and five big hens;
Them bones gonna rise again!

Them bones gonna rise again,
Them bones gonna rise again,
I knows it, indeed I knows it, brother,
Them bones gonna rise again!

Peanut Butter and Jelly

Click on the beat and when actions are chanted make the actions in time with the beat.

      ☆   ☆
1   Pea-nut,
        ☆   ☆
2   peanut butter — and jelly
      ☆   ☆
1   Pea-nut,
        ☆   ☆
2   peanut butter — and jelly
      ☆   ☆
1   Pea-nut,
        ☆   ☆
2   peanut butter — and jelly

1   First you take a peanut
2   and you smush it   *(hammer a fist shape*
ALL You smush it,   *into your palm on the beat)*

1   Pea-nut,
2   peanut butter — and jelly
1   Pea-nut,
2   pea-nut butter — and jelly
1   Pea-nut,
2   peanut butter — and jelly.

1   Then you use a knife   *(use hands to make a*
2   to spread it,   *spreading action*
ALL Spread it.   *on the beat)*
1   Then you use a knife
2   to spread it,
ALL Spread it.

1	Pea-nut,
2	peanut butter — and jelly
1	Pea-nut,
2	peanut butter — and jelly
1	Pea-nut,
2	peanut butter — and jelly

1	Then you make a sandwich	*(clap hands on the*
2	a sandwich.	*beat)*
1	Then you make a sandwich	
ALL	a sandwich.	

1	Pea-nut,
2	peanut butter — and jelly
1	Pea-nut,
2	peanut butter — and jelly
1	Pea-nut,
2	peanut butter — and jelly.

ALL   THEN YOU EAT IT!

Chicken in the Bread Tray

This chant is in two parts. Group A, or half the group begins, and speaks in a child's voice asking a question. The other half, group B, is Auntie and has a grouchy adult voice. All voices join together on lines three and four. Line four is very loud.

GROUP A	Auntie, will your dog bite?
GROUP B	No, child, no!
ALL	Chicken in the bread tray,
ALL (LOUD)	**Making up dough.**

Auntie will your broom hit?
Yes, child, pop!
Chicken in the bread tray,
Flop! Flop! Flop!

Auntie will your oven bake?
Yes, just try!
What's that chicken good for?
Pie! Pie! Pie!

Auntie, is your pie good?
Good as you can expect!
Chicken in the bread tray
Peck! Peck! Peck!

I Went Upstairs

*This is chanted in two parts. One person chants the lead
voice and the rest of the group join in on the group voice.
Clap or click on the* ●

LEAD VOICE   I went upstairs to make my bed

GROUP VOICE   And by mistake he bumped his head.

I went downstairs to cook my food
And by mistake he cooked his shoe.

I went downstairs to hang some clothes
And by mistake he hung his toes.

I went downstairs to milk my cow
And by mistake he milked the sow.

I went into the kitchen to bake a pie
And by mistake he baked a fly.

Who you gonna marry?
Buck Jones.

What you gonna feed him?
Neck bones.

Who you gonna marry?
Johnny Mack Brown.

Where you gonna live?
Downtown.

Pig Ignorant

Colin McNaughton

This chant is for two voices. Alternatively, a lead voice could read the words in plain text and a group voice read the words in **bold***.*

When I was small, I had a pig.
No you didn't!
Yes I did!

He wore a powdered periwig.
No he didn't!
Yes he did!

He wore a suit of royal blue silk.
No he didn't!
Yes he did!

And dined on plums and buttermilk.
No he didn't!
Yes he did!

He slept each night on a featherbed.
No he didn't!
Yes he did!

With a fancy hat upon his head.
He didn't did he?
Yes he did!

He'd ride a bicycle to town.
He didn't did he?
Yes he did!

Just to knock the butcher down.
He didn't did he?
Yes he did!

My pig would jump from the roof of his sty.
Did he really?
Yes he did!

Flap his ears and pigs would fly.
Did he really?
Yes he did!

If this is true, this story's big!
Well believe it or not. I don't care a fig!
Not a word of a lie, from the plums to the wig?
Nothing but the truth. (Except the bit about the pig.)

Chants For More Voices

Way Down South

This chant is spoken by three groups or three individual readers. All join in on line four.

A   Way down south where bananas grow,
B   A fly stepped on an elephant's toe.
C   The elephant cried with tears in his eyes,
ALL   **'Why don't you pick on someone your own size?'**

I asked my mother for fifty cents
To see the elephant jump the fence.
He jumped so high, he reached the sky,
And didn't get down till the Fourth of July.

I asked my mother for fifty more
To see the elephant scrub the floor.
He scrubbed so slow he stubbed his toe,
And that was the end of the elephant show.

I Went To The Animal Fair

This can be chanted as a round. Reader one or group one begins and reader two starts from the beginning when reader one starts the second line. Reader three begins when the first reader is on line three. Up to four groups or four readers can join in the round.

1   I went to the animal fair,

2   All the birds and the beasts were there,

3   The big baboon by the light of the moon

4   Was combing his auburn hair.

1   The monkey fell from his bunk

2   And dropped on the elephant's trunk.

3   The elephant sneezed, and went down on his knees

ALL   And what became of the mon-key, mon-key, mon-key, mon-key, monk?

Bananas and Cream

David McCord

This chant can be read in four groups or with four individual readers. All join in on the chorus. Add claps to keep the rhythm.

ALL
> Bananas and cream,
> Bananas and cream:
> All we could say was
> Bananas and cream.

READER ONE   We couldn't say fruit,
READER TWO   We wouldn't say cow,
READER THREE   We didn't say sugar
READER FOUR   We don't say it now.

> Bananas and cream,
> Bananas and cream:
> All we could shout was
> Bananas and cream.

We didn't say why,
We didn't say how;
We forgot it was fruit,
We forgot the old cow;
We never said sugar,
We only said WOW!

Bananas and cream
Bananas and cream
All that we want is
Bananas and cream!

We didn't say dish,
We didn't say spoon;
We said not tomorrow,
But NOW and HOW SOON.

Bananas and cream
Bananas and cream?
We yelled for bananas,
Bananas and scream!

Said the Boy to the Dinosaur

Colin McNaughton

This chant has four parts. One group can read the first line of each verse. The second group reads the line spoken by the boy. The third group reads line three and the fourth line is spoken by the dinosaur. The class can work out who reads verses six and seven as these do not fit the pattern.

Said the boy to the dinosaur:
'Outa my way!'
Said the dinosaur:
'That's not a nice thing to say.'

Said the boy to the dinosaur:
'Go take a hike!'
Said the dinosaur:
'Not an expression I like.'

Said the boy to the dinosaur:
'Move aside Mac!'
Said the dinosaur:
'Obviously manners you lack.'

Said the boy to the dinosaur:
'Go fly a kite!'
Said the dinosaur:
'That's what I call impolite.'

Said the boy to the dinosaur:
'Jump in the lake!'
Said the dinosaur:
'That's as much as I'll take!'

The monster was cross,
Which is what you'd expect;

'I'm older than you,
You should show some respect!'

He taught him a lesson,
What more can I say?
The dinosaur ate him
And went on his way.

The Trouble With My Brother

Brian Patten

This poem can be chanted by individual readers reading
one verse each. All join in on the chorus printed in bold
type.

READER 1	Thomas was only three
READER 2	And though he was not fat
READER 3	We knew that there was something wrong
ALL	When he ate the cat.

ALL	**Nibble, nibble, munch, munch,**
	Nibble, nibble, munch,
	Nibble, nibble, munch, munch,
READER 1	He had the cat for lunch!

He ate a lump of coal,
He ate a candlestick
And when he ate the tortoise
Mother felt quite sick.

Nibble, nibble, munch, munch,
Nibble, nibble, munch,
Nibble, nibble, munch, munch,
A tortoise for lunch!

When he was a boy of four
He went to the zoo by bus
And alarmed us all by eating
A hippopotamus.

Nibble, nibble, munch, munch,
Nibble, nibble, munch,
Nibble, nibble, munch, munch,
A hippopotamus for lunch!

When he went to school
We tried to warn the teacher
But Thomas pounced long before
Anyone could reach her.

Nibble, nibble, munch, munch,
Nibble, nibble, munch,
Nibble, nibble, munch, munch,
A teacher for lunch!

We used to get nice letters
So mum was full of grief
When upon the doorstep
She found the postman's teeth.

Nibble, nibble, munch, munch,
Nibble, nibble, munch,
Nibble, nibble, munch, munch,
A postman for lunch!

Absolute Nonsense

These chants may have claps, clicks, footstamps and other sound effects. Individual children or groups of readers may be used to perform the chants.

Who's Been Sleeping in My Porridge?

Colin McNaughton

Characters: Goldilocks, Mummy Bear, Papa Bear, Baby Bear and a narrator to read the indirect speech.

'Who's been sitting in my bed?'
said the mummy bear crossly.

'Who's been eating my chair?'
said the baby bear weepily.

'Who's been sleeping in my porridge?'
said the papa bear angrily.

'Wait a minute,' said Goldilocks.
'Why can't you guys just stick to the script?
Now let's try it again and this time no messing about.'

Muvver's Lament

GROUP A   A muvver was washing her baby one night
GROUP B   The youngest of ten and a delicate mite.
GROUP A   The muvver was poor and the baby was fin
GROUP B   T'was naught but a skellington
GROUP A   Covered wiv skin

GROUP A   The muvver turned round for the soap off the rack.
GROUP B   She was only a moment but when she turned back
GROUP B   Her baby was gone and in anguish she cried
GROUP B   Oh, where has my baby gone?
GROUP A   The Angels replied.

ALL
(Chorus)   'Oh, your baby has gone down the plug-hole. (the plug hole)
Your baby has gone down the plug.
The poor little fing was so skinny and fin
It should have been washed in a jug (a jug?)
Your baby is perfectly happy.
He won't need a bath anymore.
He's muckin' about wiv angels above
Not lost but gone before.

Nickety Nackety Now Now Now

Adapted by Susan Hill

*The original version of Nickety Nackety Now Now Now had the wife doing all the work, so a new version was created here. Children could invent more verses. A group voice chants **Nickety, nackety, now, now now!** Clap loudly on **now, now, now.***

46

LEAD	I married my wife in the month of June
GROUP	**Nickety, nackety, now, now, now!**
LEAD	I escorted her home by the light of the moon.
	Nickety, nackety nay down thackety!
	Willity, wallity, rustico quality!
GROUP	**Nickety, nackety, now, now, now!**

'One day when I came in from the plow,'
Nickety, nackety, now, now, now!
Says, 'Oh, my good wife, is my dinner ready now?'
Nickety, nackety nay down thackety!
Willity, wallity, rustico quality!
Nickety, nackety, now, now, now!

'There's a little piece of corn bread on the shelf,'
Nickety, nackety, now, now, now!
'If you want anymore you can bake it yourself.'
Nickety, nackety nay down thackety!
Willity, wallity, rustico quality!
Nickety, nackety, now, now, now!

Says, 'I work all day and into the night'
Nickety, nackety, now, now, now!
'Is it too much to ask for a bite?'
Nickety, nackety nay down thackety!
Willity, wallity, rustico quality!
Nickety, nackety, now, now, now!

'Do you think all I do all day is sleep?'
Nickety, nackety, now, now, now!
I look after twelve children who make me weep!'
Nickety, nackety nay down thackety!
Willity, wallity, rustico quality!
Nickety, nackety, now, now, now!

'Out to work those children go.'
Nickety, nackety, now, now, now!
'We'll sit home and collect the dough.'
Nickety, nackety nay down thackety!
Willity, wallity, rustico quality!
Nickety, nackety, now, now, now!

A Dark, Dark World

READER 1	In the **dark, dark** world
READER 1,2	There's a **dark, dark** country
READER 1,2,3	In the **dark, dark** country
READER 1-4	There's a **dark, dark** wood
READER 1-5	In the **dark, dark** wood
READER 1-6	There's a **dark, dark** house
READER 1-7	In the **dark, dark** house
READER 1-8	There's a person trying to mend a fuse.

If You Ever

This is a nonsense chant, a tongue twister, so try to say it quickly.

If you ever ever ever ever ever
If you ever ever ever meet a whale
You must never never never never never
Touch his tail:

For if you ever ever ever ever ever
If you ever ever ever touch his tail
You will never never never never never
You will never never never meet another whale.

Mrs McPhee

Charles Causley

This is a clapping chant. Clap, click or footstamp on the beat. Select one group to make quacking sounds on the beat. These quacking sounds become louder and louder until a shout at the end of the chant.

Mrs McPhee
Who lived in South Zeal
Roasted a duckling
For every meal.

'Duckling for breakfast
And dinner and tea
And duckling for supper,'
Said Mrs McPhee.

'It's sweeter than sugar,
It's clean as a nut,
I'm sure and I'm certain
It's good for me — BUT

'I don't like these feathers
That grow down my back,
And my silly webbed feet
And my voice that goes quack.'

As easy and soft
As a ship in the sea,
As a duck to the water
Went Mrs McPhee.

'I think I'll go swim
In the river,' said she;
Said Mrs Mac, Mrs Quack,
Mrs McPhee.

Rockin' Robin

J. Thomas

Group A chants the words in plain text. Group B the words in bold. Group C clicks, claps or uses body percussion like foot stamps, tongue clicks or mouth pops on the beat.

(chorus)
Twidderlee didderlee dee — **Twidderlee didderlee dee**
Twidderlee didderlee dee — **Twidderlee didderlee dee**
Twidderlee didderlee dee — **Twidderlee didderlee dee**
Tweet! Tweet — **Tweet! Tweet**

He rocks in the tree-tops all day long,
Hoppin' and a boppin' and a singin' this song.
All the little birdies on Jay Bird Street
Love to hear that robin goin' 'Tweet Tweet Tweet'
Rockin' robin **(tweet tweet twidderlee tweet)**
Rockin' robin **(tweet tweet twidderlee tweet)**
Blow rockin' robin 'cause you're really goin' to rock tonight.

(chorus)

Every little swallow, every chickadee,
Every little bird in the tall oak tree,
The wise old owl, the big black crow,
Flappin' their wings, singin' 'Go bird go!'
Rockin' robin **(tweet tweet twidderlee tweet)**
Rockin' robin **(tweet tweet twidderlee tweet)**
Blow rockin' robin 'cause your'e really goin' to rock tonight.

(chorus)

A pretty little raven at the bandstand
Taught him how to do the bop and it was grand
They started goin' steady and a-bless my soul
He out-bopped the buzzard and the oriole.

(chorus)

Yooowll-lee!

*This chant was adapted from the traditional chant Fiddle-i-
fee! A different reader reads each new character. Readers
all join in on the chorus once their animal has been called.*

READER 1: I had a little dingo and the dingo loved me,
I fed my dingo under yonder tree.
Dingo went 'Yooowll-lee!'

READER 2: I had a little kangaroo and the 'roo loved me,
I fed my 'roo under yonder tree.
Roo went 'Chug-a-lug, chug-a-lug!'

Dingo went 'Yooowll-lee!'

READER 3:   I had a little emu and the emu loved me,
I fed my emu under yonder tree.
Emu went 'Tug-a-lugga, tugga-a-lugga!'
Roo went 'Chug-a-lug, chug-a-lug!'
Dingo went 'Yooowll-lee!'

I had a little snake and the snake loved me,
I fed my snake under yonder tree.
Snake went 'Issy-hissy, issy-hissy!'
Emu went 'Tug-a-lugga, tugga-a-lugga!'
Roo went 'Chug-a-lug, chug-a-lug!'
Dingo went 'Yooowll-lee!'

I had a little kookaburra, and the kookaburra
loved me,
I fed my kookaburra under yonder tree.
Kookaburra went 'A-ha-ha!'
Snake went 'Issy-hissy, Issy-hissy!'
Emu went 'Tug-a-lugga, tug-a-lugga!'
Roo went 'Chug-a-lug, chug-a-lug!'
Dingo went 'Yooowll-lee!'

I had a little possum and the possum loved me,
I fed my possum under yonder tree.
Possum went 'Cus-cus, cus-cus!'
Kookaburra went 'A-ha-ha!'
Snake went 'Issy-hissy, Issy-hissy!'
Emu went 'Tug-a-lugga, tug-a-lugga!'
Roo went 'Chug-a-lug, chug-a-lug!'
Dingo went 'Yooowll-lee!'

I had a little wombat and the wombat loved me,
I fed my wombat under yonder tree.
Wombat went 'Snuffle-snuffle!'
Possum went 'Cus-cus, cus-cus!'
Kookaburra went 'A-ha-ha!'
Snake went 'Issy-hissy, Issy-hissy!'
Emu went 'Tug-a-lugga, tug-a-lugga!'
Roo went 'Chug-a-lug, chug-a-lug!'
Dingo went 'Yooowll-lee!';

I had a little parrrot and the parrot loved me,
I fed my parrot under yonder tree.
Parrot went 'Pretty boy, pretty boy!'
Wombat went 'Snuffle-snuffle!'
Possum went 'Cus-cus, cus-cus!',
Kookaburra went 'A-ha-ha!'
Snake went 'Issy-hissy, Issy-hissy!'
Emu went 'Tug-a-lugga, tug-a-lugga!'
Roo went 'Chug-a-lug, chug-a-lug!'
Dingo went 'Yooowll-lee!'

I had a little crocodile and the croc loved me,
I fed my croc under yonder tree.
Croc went- 'SNAP-SNAP, SNAP-SNAP,
SNAP-SNAP, SNAP!'

(and all jump up.)

'Quack', Said the Billy Goat

Charles Causley

This chant is sheer nonsense. Animal sounds are mixed up and out of character. Assign twelve readers to read the sounds the animals make. The rest of the group can read the text that is not in quotation marks.

'Quack!' said the billy-goat.
'Oink!' said the hen.
'Miaow!' said the little chick
Running in the pen.
'Hobble-gobble!' said the dog.
'Cluck!' said the sow.
'Tu-whit Tu-whoo!' the donkey said.
'Baa!' said the cow.
'Hee-haw!' the turkey cried.
The duck began to moo.
All at once the sheep went,
'Cock-a-doodle-doo!'
The owl coughed and cleared his throat
And began to bleat.
'Bow-wow!' said the cock'
Swimming in the leat.
'Cheep-cheep!' said the cat
As she began to fly.
'Farmer's been and laid an egg —
That's the reason why!'

I'm Gargling In The Rain

Colin McNaughton

(to the tune of Singing in the Rain)

Do be do do, do be, do be do do
I'm singing in the rain
Just singing in the rain
Gargle glorious feeling
Glub gargle again.
Blargle glargle gargle glog,
Blar — blargle, glub gargle in the rain

Acknowledgements

The author and publisher thank the following copyright holders for permission to reprint material in this book. If any errors in acknowledgements have occurred they were inadvertent and will be corrected in subsequent editions as they are brought to their notice. Every effort has been made to acquire permission for the use of this material.

'Food' and 'My Little Sister' from *Smile Please* by Tony Bradman, copyright © Tony Bradman, 1987. Published by Viking Children's Books

'Feeding the Family' and 'Trouble With My Brother' from *Gargling With Jelly* by Brian Patten, copyright © Brian Patten, 1985. Published by Viking Children's Books. U.S. rights by permission of Roger Coleridge & White Ltd.

'Quack Said the Billy Goat' and 'Mrs McPhee' from *Early in the Morning* by Charles Causley, copyright © Charles Causley. Published by Penguin UK.

'Rockin' Robin' by J Thomas permission granted by J Albert and Son.

'Pig Ignorant', 'Said the Boy to the Dinosaur', 'Who's Been Sleeping in My Porridge?' and 'I'm Gargling in the Rain'

References

Roger D Abrahams (1969) *Jump-Rope Rhymes: a Dictionary* (ed) American Folklore Society, University of Texas Press

Tony Bradman (1987) *Smile Please*, Puffin

Dorothy Butler (1983) *For Me, Me, Me; Poems for the Very Young* Hodder and Stoughton

Charles Causley (1986) *Early in the Morning;* A collection of new poems Viking Kestrel

Richard Chase (1956) *American Folktales and Songs*, New American Library

Harold Courlander (1963) *Negro Folk Music USA* Columbia University Press

Alice Bertha (1964) *Traditional Games of England, Scotland and Ireland* Vol 2 Dover Publications NY

L Goss and M Barnes (1989) *Talk that Talk: an Anthology of African-American Storytelling.* A Touchstone Book Simon and Schuster

Barbara Michels and Bettye White (1983) *Apples on a stick: The Folklore of Black Children* Coward-McCann

Colin McNaughton (1992) *Who's Been Sleeping in My Porridge? A Book of Daft Poems and Pictures*, Walker Books

Iona and Peter Opie, (1959) *Lore and Language of School Children*, Clarendon Press

Patten, Brian (1985) *Gargling with Jelly*, Puffin, UK